Rookie
Read-About® Geography

Michigan

By Jan Mader

Consultant
Jeanne Clidas, Ph.D.
National Reading Consultant
and
Professor of Reading, SUNY Brockport

Children's Press®
A Division of Scholastic Inc.
New York Toronto London Auckland Sydney
Mexico City New Delhi Hong Kong
Danbury, Connecticut

Designer: Herman Adler Design
Photo Researcher: Caroline Anderson
The photo on the cover shows Wagner Falls.

Library of Congress Cataloging-in-Publication Data

Mader, Jan.
  Michigan / by Jan Mader.
    p. cm. – (Rookie read-about geography)
  Includes index.
  Summary: A simple introduction to Michigan, focusing on its geographical features and points of interest.
  ISBN 0-516-22736-X (lib. bdg.)   0-516-27781-2 (pbk.)
  1. Michigan–Juvenile literature. 2. Michigan–Geography–Juvenile literature. [1. Michigan.] I. Title. II. Series.
  F566.3 .M23 2003
  917.74—dc21
                                                      2002011561

©2003 Children's Press
A Division of Scholastic Inc.
All rights reserved. Published simultaneously in Canada.
Printed in China.

CHILDREN'S PRESS, AND ROOKIE READ-ABOUT®,
and associated logos are trademarks and or registered trademarks
of Grolier Publishing Co., Inc. SCHOLASTIC and associated logos
are trademarks and or registered trademarks of Scholastic Inc.
3 4 5 6 7 8 9 10 R 12 11 10 09 08 07

Do you know which state is shaped like a mitten?

It is Michigan!

Michigan has two parts called the Upper Peninsula and the Lower Peninsula.

A peninsula (puh-NIN-suh-luh) has water on three sides of the land. The Lower Peninsula is shaped like a mitten.

You must cross the Mackinac Bridge to get from one peninsula to the other.

Michigan is known as the Great Lakes State. It touches Lake Superior, Lake Huron, Lake Erie (EE-ree), and Lake Michigan.

Some people fish and play in the lakes.

There are big ships called freighters (FRAY-turz) on the lakes. They move steel, cars, and many other things to places far away.

This is one of the ways people use the lakes to help them work.

People in Michigan do many kinds of work. They work in offices, stores, schools, and banks. Some people work on farms.

Some people in Michigan may work in factories making cars.

Detroit is a big city in Michigan. It is known as "Motor City" because so many cars are made there.

You can see how cars used to look in Dearborn, Michigan. You will find the Henry Ford Museum (myoo-ZEE-um) there. A museum is a place people go to look at interesting things.

Henry Ford invented one of the first cars.

19

Half of Michigan is covered with forests. Many animals live in the forests.

The state bird of Michigan is the robin.

Have you ever heard Michigan called the "Wolverine (WUL-vuh-reen) State"?

Trappers used to catch these small animals and trade their furs. There are no wolverines in Michigan now. Their relatives are the muskrats, beavers, badgers, and weasels. These animals still live there.

The University of Michigan is in Ann Arbor. The football team is called the Michigan Wolverines.

Winters in the Upper Peninsula can be very cold.

Summers in the Lower Peninsula are warm. The land in the Lower Peninsula is good for growing fruit.

27

The children in Michigan love the snow. Sledding and skiing are great fun!

What would you like to see and do in Michigan?

Words You Know

beaver

factory

freighter

Henry Ford Museum   lake

Mackinac Bridge   robin

Index

animals 20, 21, 22, 24
cars 15, 18, 30
climate 26, 27, 28
Dearborn 18
Detroit ("Motor City") 16
Great Lakes 9, 10, 13
Henry Ford Museum 18, 31
Lower Peninsula 5, 27
Mackinac Bridge 6, 7
maps 4, 8
Upper Peninsula 5, 26
wolverines, "Wolverine State" 22, 24

About the Author

Jan Mader has been writing for children for 15 years. Her natural curiosity and joy of life characterize her work in more than 24 published easy-reader stories.

Photo Credits

Photographs © 2003: AP/Wide World Photos/Doug Bauman/The Oakland Press: 14; Dembinsky Photo Assoc.: 26 (Claudia Adams), 23, 30 top left (Dominique Braud), 29 (Gary Bublitz), cover (Barbara Gerlach), 24 (Stephen Graham), 16 (Doug Locke), 21, 31 bottom right (Gary Meszaros), 7, 31 bottom left (Skip Moody), 17; Folio, Inc./David R. Frazier: 27; Getty Images/Brent Smith/Reuters: 25; Peter Arnold Inc.: 20 (Ed Reschke), 10 (Carl R. Sams II); PhotoEdit/Barbara Stizer: 3; Stone/Getty Images/Vito Palmisano: 11, 31 top right; Superstock, Inc.: 15, 19, 30 top right, 31 top left; The Image Works: 12, 30 bottom (Townsend P. Dickinson), 19 inset (Topham).

Maps by Bob Italiano